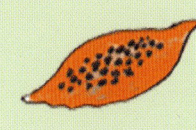

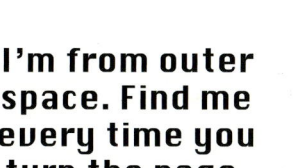

I'm from outer space. Find me every time you turn the page, earthlings!

FOOD FOR ALL

What we eat and where it comes from

WORDS BY MARY HOFFMAN
PICTURES BY ROS ASQUITH

Otter-Barry BOOKS

For Rowan Coutts and Lyla Granatstein – MH
For Theo, Olympia and Atalanti – RA

Text copyright © Mary Hoffman 2025
Illustrations copyright © Ros Asquith 2025

First published in Great Britain in 2025 by Otter-Barry Books, Little Orchard,
Burley Gate, Herefordshire, HR1 3QS

Information sources for Food for All include:
Ravenous by Henry Dimbleby (Profile Books, 2022), *Ultra Processed People* by Chris van Tulleken
(Cornerstone Press, 2023), *Food for Life* by Tim Spector (Jonathan Cape, 2022), National Geographic,
Food and Agricultural Organisation of the United Nations

www.
otterbarrybooks.
com

Illustrated in pen, ink
and watercolour

LESS
SUGAR

Set in
Brandon
Grotesque

ISBN
978-1-915659-
37-8

Printed in
China

I LOVE
PEAS

MIX
Paper | Supporting
responsible forestry
FSC
www.fsc.org
FSC® C104723

Contents

EAT WELL

NO WASTE

SLOW FOOD

Words by

Otter-Barry BOOKS

Mary Hoffman

Pictures by

Ros Asquith

Food, glorious food!

Food! Who doesn't like it? Every creature in the world from a tiny caterpillar to a tiger, to a great blue whale, needs some kind of food in order to live.

Some eat just grass or plants, some eat fish or other sea creatures. And some, including many humans, eat other animals.

Strange that the biggest creature on your planet, the blue whale, eats one of the tiniest, krill.

KRILL

I'm only 2cm long, yet this whale is 29 metres.

I'm a vegetarian.

I eat everything!

Does a very hungry caterpillar eat more than a butterfly?

Many living creatures, like very small birds or sheep and cows, have to spend most of the day eating to get enough energy.

Growing food

There are six main crops grown on the land - wheat, rice, maize, potatoes, cassava and sweet potatoes. Then there are all the other fruits and vegetables that we eat.

HUMANS EAT

Cereals
Pulses
Roots
Fruits
Fish
Dairy
Meat
Nuts
Eggs
Vegetables

Isn't it weird to feed the animals plants, then eat the animals? Why not just eat the plants?

Farmers plant crops in their fields for human food and grow grass for animals to eat.

Too much of our planet is now given over to growing food for people and animals.

We need our trees and forests to keep the air we breathe clean. So, if they are cut down to make way for fields of grass, it increases pollution and adds to climate change. But many farmers are beginning to realise this and manage the land better.

If people don't eat so many of us...

there will be more trees.

More birds too!

And cleaner air for us to breathe.

What plants need

All plants need water and sunlight in order to grow. Farmers often speed up the growth of plants by using chemical fertilisers, but these cause problems when rain washes them into the rivers, polluting the water and harming wildlife.

More chemicals can be used to kill pests on crops, like insects which eat the growing plants, but they also harm birds and other wildlife. And getting chemicals into our food and water means we end up eating them too.

But there are also organic farms, which don't use chemicals on the growing food.

Do you have any pizza seeds?

What animals need

Animals raised for us to eat need their own food. It might be just grass or it might be oats, alfalfa, barley, corn or hay (which is long grass dried by the sun). And the animals need to be well looked-after and to have a good life.

Perhaps you don't treat animals well enough because you are just going to eat them!

Eggs can come from hens who are allowed to range freely but they are cheaper when they come from hens who live a hard life, squashed close together in a big building with no room to roam around. This is called 'factory farming', treating chickens and other animals like machines instead of living creatures.

'Free-range' eggs mean hens have a better life.

I only eat free-range mice.

Cheaper eggs may be called 'Farm-fresh' but they are factory farmed.

There are some laws about how to treat animals who become our food, but the law doesn't go far enough to make sure all animals have a good life.

Sadly, factory farming
squashes animals together.

But there are many farmers who are
treating animals well, so they look more like
happy creatures from a picture book.

Harvest

All the crops that people grow have to be harvested, whether they are wheat, rice, fruit or hay for animal feed. The crops must be ripe before they can be picked or cut and this happens at different times of year for different plants and in different countries.

Crops like wheat are usually harvested by big machines and stored in giant barns. Fruits like berries and olives are usually picked by hand and need a lot of workers to do the job.

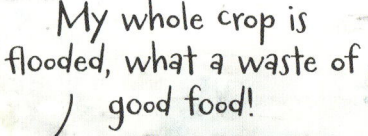

My whole crop is flooded, what a waste of good food!

It's not very well paid and so there might be a shortage of hands to do the work. When this happens, the crop may be left to rot and not end up on our plates at all.

If the weather has been bad – too hot and dry or too wet – then the crop can't be harvested, so that food is lost too.

It's a pity you humans don't eat mice when there are so many of them around at harvest-time.

But when the harvest is good, everyone is happy and wants to celebrate because there will be enough food for the next year.

In India we have over 20 harvest festivals.

These festivals are from Kerala, Assam and Ladakh.

What we get from animals

Plants are not the only source of food for most people. If you are not vegan, you will eat cheese and yoghurt and cream and drink milk. These are known as dairy foods and come from cows, goats or sheep. Vegetarians will eat eggs too, which come from chickens.

If you are vegan, there are dairy substitutes for milk, cheese and yoghurt and even for eggs.

And then there is meat. Meat is the flesh or organs of animals and so the animals have to be killed to provide us with meat to eat. This is why some people choose to be vegans or vegetarians.

But the majority of people do eat meat and fish, so big businesses have grown up to provide them, raising animals, 'farming' or catching fish, and then killing them, cutting them up and getting them to supermarkets, butchers and fishmongers for people to buy and cook.

MILK

milk, cheese, butter,

We give them eggs,

Do the animals know you are going to eat them?

Doctor, can you make me taste like old socks?

That's what happens in rich countries and in cities across the world. In poorer countries people in rural areas may raise their own chickens, pigs and goats, or fish in local rivers and seas. It may be that those animals have a better life.

yoghurt,

wool,

and then they EAT US!

How does food get to us?

It's a huge business to get crops and meat and fish and dairy foods from where they begin to the shops, markets and supermarkets where people can buy them.

The food has to be transported, most of it in refrigerated lorries, and then may be taken by planes to other countries. The UK exports some of its food, but about 40% comes from other places in the world.

Do you fancy Spain or Majorca this year?

Potato Holidays

FAMILY ROAST DINNER

Nothing like a lovely British roast dinner!

The lamb's from New Zealand,

the potatoes are from Majorca,

and the peas are French.

Just as with harvesting, distributing food can be affected by weather or wars or natural disasters. The more dependent a country is on food that comes from outside it, the less safe the food supply is and the country is more at risk of shortages – or even famine.

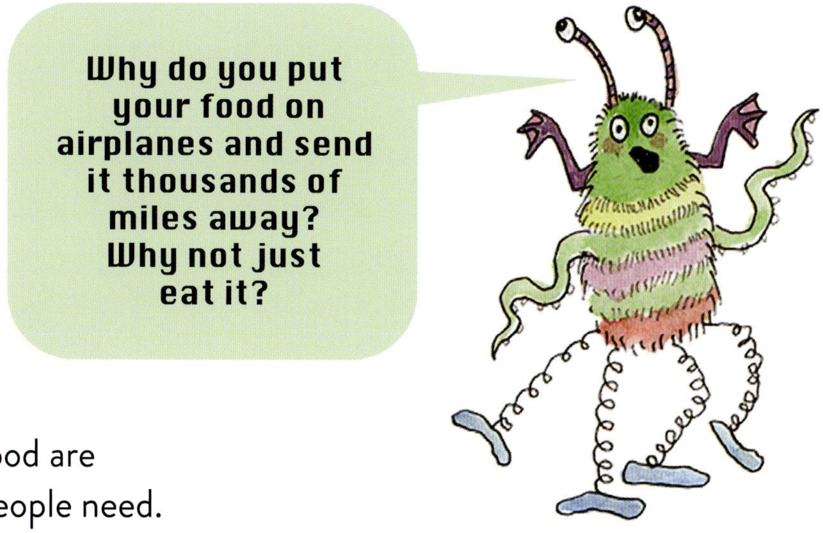
Why do you put your food on airplanes and send it thousands of miles away? Why not just eat it?

Countries that produce most of their own food are much more secure in supplying what their people need.

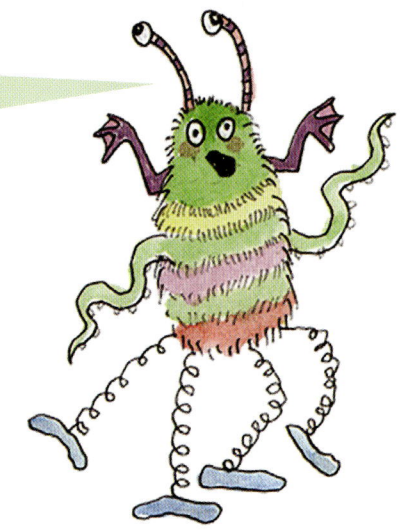

THE SAME FAMILY ONE YEAR LATER

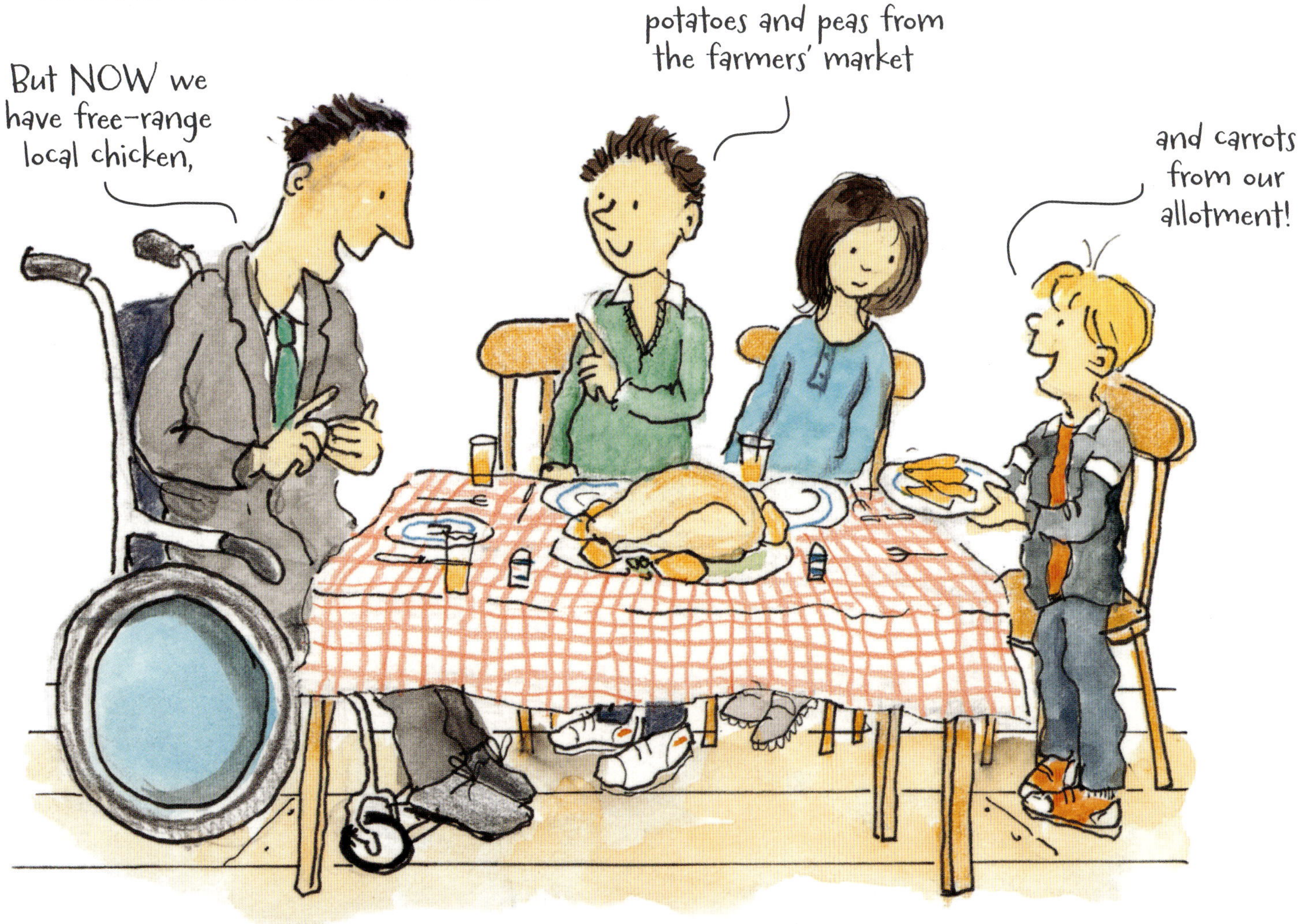
But NOW we have free-range local chicken,
potatoes and peas from the farmers' market
and carrots from our allotment!

Shopping

Why do most of you grow flowers in your gardens when you can't eat them?

Who does the shopping in your family? In the developed world, most people get their food from supermarkets, whether by going there in person or ordering a delivery online.

No wonder this pear is mouldy, it's flown halfway around the world to get here.

Home-grown Tomatoes

Imported Tomatoes

These cost more. Why?

But there are still smaller local shops like bakers and butchers and greengrocers. And many towns and villages still have fresh food markets where you go in person and choose what you buy from individual stalls.

Some people grow their own fruit and vegetables, in gardens and allotments. They may keep chickens for their eggs or a goat for milk and cheese.

With a greenhouse and a polytunnel you can grow almost anything in the UK!

Not coconuts or papaya!

WINDOW BOX FARMERS' MARKET

The fresher our food is, the tastier and the better for us it is too. But most of us who live in towns and cities will buy some food at the supermarket that has come a long way from where it was grown.

To help cut down on 'food miles', we can look at where the food comes from and decide not to buy the things that come from thousands of miles away.

What can you eat?

Some people are fussy about their food – not just children! There are grown-ups who won't eat vegetables, while others don't like food of particular colours.

For other people there are foods that they can't absorb or are allergic to. A small number can be made very ill, or even die from eating the wrong foods for them.

People who are allergic to nuts need medical help the minute they eat one by mistake. People with coeliac disease are made very ill by gluten, a protein found in wheat and some other grains, which is in bread, cakes, biscuits and pasta.

I'll eat anything beginning with P as long as it's pasta.

He says he can't eat this. Can you get his teacher?

Why? She won't eat it either!

You earthlings certainly spend a lot of time deciding what to eat.

But to choose what you eat is a luxury. It's only possible if you have enough food and are not starving. If there is plenty to go round, you may then choose to eat only what you like. And you might choose to be vegetarian or vegan.

You may have heard the words 'a balanced diet'. You can probably guess this means not munching only crisps and chocolate all day. Let's see what it really means....

EAT LESS BEEF

Well, he would say that wouldn't he?

A balanced diet

Different food groups provide us with different things our bodies need to grow and stay healthy.

Carbohydrates, which provide energy, are found in bread, cakes, rice, pasta, noodles and many other delicious foods.

We need more sweets on the left.

A BALANCED DIET

Protein, which builds muscles, comes from meat, fish, eggs, cheese, milk, yoghurt, lentils, soybeans, nuts and processed food like tofu (made from soya) and Quorn (made from something a bit like mushrooms).
Fats, which keep our bodies running – our hair and skin and our bodies' cells – are found in oils, butter, and some meat and fish.

Wow, it's complicated on earth! On my planet there are only two things to eat.

Vitamins and minerals, which we also need, are in all sorts of food, especially in green vegetables and fruits. A balanced diet should contain elements of all these food groups, either every day or at every meal.

Do I have a chocolate deficiency?

No!

DOCTOR

Vitamins

A carrots   cheese   Eggs

B peas   nuts   wholemeal bread

C potatoes   berries   broccoli

D oily fish   red meat   egg yolk

E nuts & seeds   milk   avocado

K green leafy veg   vegetable oil   cereal

You can get vitamin D from sunlight too!

Sugar is found naturally in fruit and honey but is also made from sugar-cane plants or sugar beets.

Although lots of people enjoy sugar in cakes and sweets and chocolate and in fizzy drinks and puddings, it is bad for our teeth and our general health and we should all eat less of it.

A lot of sugar is added by makers to foods that might surprise you, like peanut butter, bread and yoghurt and ready meals. We really don't need added sugar even though it's tasty.

I'm going sugar free.

Cooking

Some foods can be eaten without any cooking – fruit, nuts, seeds, cheese and salad vegetables like tomatoes and lettuces. But most people want a hot meal every day, if they can get it. So who cooks the food in your family?

HOW TO MAKE TOAST

HOW TO BOIL AN EGG

HOW TO MAKE TEA

Some people don't know how to cook so they buy ready-made meals or takeaways, which are expensive.

Others can't afford the cost of the gas or electricity needed to cook the food. And for many people round the world, cooking a meal would be a luxury.

Cooking is not difficult, the way some TV chefs make it seem, but it does take time and you need to learn a few basic skills. If your mum or dad is a good cook, ask them to teach you. It's a wonderful thing to be able to feed a family with just a few ingredients.

My best dishes are Apple Pie and Sausage Casserole.

Which is this?

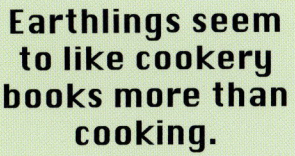

Earthlings seem to like cookery books more than cooking.

Then there is cooking for special days, like baking a birthday cake or making a Christmas dinner or the first meal after Ramadan.

What would you like someone to cook for you?

Processing and packaging

Almost all food goes through some processes before it reaches our tables. But some have far more than others. There is a popular and cheap cooking oil that goes through thirteen different stages in a factory before it reaches the shops. A recent list of what goes into a packaged egg mayonnaise sandwich showed 32 ingredients!

Not nutritious but very cheap.

My sandwich has lots more ingredients than yours!

That's why mine's tastier.

Why do earthlings eat so much that isn't real food?

Going through many processes and having lots of ingredients takes food further and further away from its natural sources. And this makes it less good for us to eat.

If you buy food in supermarkets, most of it is in packets and most of the packets are made of plastic. In some supermarkets even bananas, which come naturally packaged, are put in polystyrene trays covered in clingfilm.

YOU ARE WHAT YOU EAT

Plastic is so bad for the planet because it breaks down very slowly and it fills up our oceans and kills sea creatures.

We can choose not to buy highly-packaged food. But that's easier if you are the one doing the shopping or if you go shopping with your parent or carer.

So do you eat lots of bananas, Miss?

All around the world

Tea   Tee   Çaj   Té

In many countries there is one main food that people eat every day, called a 'staple'. It could be soybeans, sweet potato or plantains. Did you know that rice is a staple for half the world? But growing wheat takes up more of the Earth's land surface than any other crop. You can make it into pasta, biscuits, cakes, naan bread, chapatis, rolls and bagels.

All countries have their own national and regional dishes – paella in Spain and kebabs in Turkey, hummus in the Middle East, sushi in Japan.

Pizza is the world's favourite food!

Mine too!

Pasta -Italy

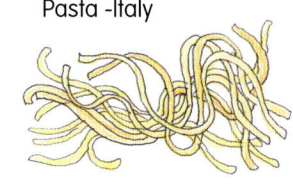

Sushi - Japan

In America, it's hamburgers, in the UK it's fish and chips. India's most popular foods are rice and lentils, samosas and pakoras.

Tacos - Mexico

Cheese - everywhere!

Paella - Spain

Moussaka - Greece

Te   Чaj   Chá   Thé   תה   شاي   Herbata   ਚਾਹ

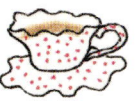  

Chai

茶

Çay

Many countries have areas where people can't afford these famous foods and struggle to get anything to eat at all.

Tea is a popular drink all over the world, and the world's favourite food is pizza! What's yours?

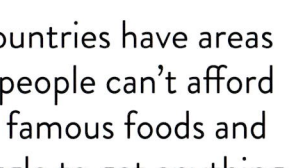
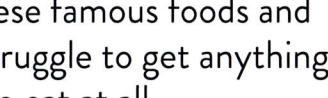

Sausages - everywhere

Ice-cream - everywhere

Borscht - Ukraine

But food is now so international that anyone in the world can eat anything, if they are lucky enough to have a choice.

Fish and Chips - UK

Hamburger - USA

My favourite food is rocks!

Goulash - Hungary

Poutine - Canada

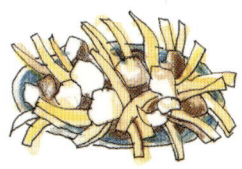

Tagine - North Africa

Pad Thai - Thailand

31

Is there enough?

My brain hurts.

Where I come from we all share our food.

There are eight billion people in the world. This jar contains eight thousand sprinkles. If each sprinkle were a person, you would need one million jars to hold them all!

SPRINKLES

There is enough food in the world, including crops and animals, to feed ten billion people. So why do one in ten people go hungry every day?

There are countries that can't grow enough food because of a lack of rain, which leads to drought. Crops and animals need water.

In some places there is too much rain, causing floods, which drown crops and animals. Or there are wars, where soldiers steal food or deliberately destroy it.

But there are other countries where there would be enough food for everyone, but the prices are so high that many people can't afford to buy it.

Help with food

Even in rich countries like the USA and UK, there are food banks, where people who can't afford to buy food can go and get it free because other people with a bit more money have given it for them.

The first food bank in the world was set up in the USA in 1967. Now there are 60,000 food banks and food pantries in the USA and over 3,000 in the UK – and more every year.

FOOD BANK

HEAT OR EAT

Why do rich earthlings need more food than poor earthlings?

A day's food for a family who has plenty.

A day's food for a family who has little.

Countries such as France and Germany also have food banks, usually supplied by local charities.

Why do we need food banks when there is enough food in the world for everyone?

Richer countries can help poorer ones by sending food or money for food when there are disasters, wars or famines.

Food waste

About a third of the food produced in the world is wasted – just thrown away. This may happen long before it reaches a shop or market, because crops are spoiled and go rotten. Or, in rich countries, people often buy more than they need and it goes bad before they can eat it.

The good news is that many countries now have food-waste collections from outside people's homes and the waste is composted to put on the land or sometimes turned into energy. As a result, food thrown away with the rubbish has gone down by about a fifth in the UK since 2007.

Climate change

The world's climate is changing – getting warmer and more unpredictable because of global warming – and this is becoming a threat to our food. Usually, if a crop fails in one part of the world because of weather (too hot or too cold, too wet or too dry), another part of the world can make up for it because it hasn't suffered any loss. But now the effects of climate change are so widespread that there is a danger of the same crop failure happening at the same time all over the world. And that would lead to terrible food shortages.

At the same time, animals like cows and sheep, who spend all day eating grass, release a gas called methane into the atmosphere, through their burps and farts and their poo.

Which is worse...

cow farts...

or car farts?

The bad thing about methane is that it contributes to global warming (but it does disperse over time in 7-12 years).

LO-FART CATTLE FOOD

So if we ate a bit less meat and had smaller or fewer herds of cows and sheep, there would be less methane in the air. And some farmers are experimenting with feeding animals supplements that prevent them producing so much methane.

My planet doesn't understand why you earthlings aren't looking after your planet.

What instead?

What can we eat instead of meat?

Meat gives us lots of first-class protein that helps build up our muscles and bones. But you can also get protein from fish, eggs, cheese, yoghurt, milk, cereals and grains, lentils, nuts, seeds and beans.

Soya beans can be processed and squeezed to produce blocks of **tofu**. It is almost tasteless, but if it is mixed with sauces and spices it makes a good meat substitute.

Maybe one day we will all eat this.

MAGIC FOOD

INGREDIENTS:
Fibre!
Proteins!
Minerals!
Oils!
NO ADDITIVES

If all the cats and dogs in the world ate vegan food, millions more people could have enough to eat.

No meat for me!

VEGAN PETS

Vegan PUSS

You earthlings seem pretty clever. Surely you can work out what to do?

In the UK a product called Quorn (see page 24), comes as chunks, fillets, mince – and even slices you can put in a sandwich.

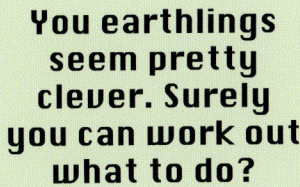

So if you want to eat foods that have a similar taste and texture to meat, there is plenty to choose from.

I need meat, fish and eggs to build my muscles.

Veggie sausages! I can't believe it's not meat!

My muscles get their protein from nuts, lentils and soya.

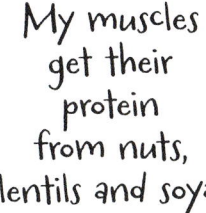

We don't need everyone to become vegan or vegetarian but it would make a big difference if people ate a bit less meat, especially from cows and sheep.

Seaweed, bugs, and more...

Lots of research is going into making new foods for us to eat in the future that are cheap to produce, not affected by weather, and high in protein.

One suggestion is to eat **seaweed**, some types of which are full of vitamins and other good things. If you have ever seen seaweed on the beach, you might not like that idea, but food made from seaweed will not look anything like the slimy green stuff you see when the tide goes out.

Another widely available source of protein is **insects**. In some countries in Africa and Asia these are already part of the human diet. People say that insects like crickets, when deep-fried, taste a bit like prawns. How would you feel about eating insects?

There is also a useful 'false banana' tree. The '**enset**' is a relative of the banana, grown in Ethiopia. The roots and pulp of just fifteen plants could feed a person for a year.

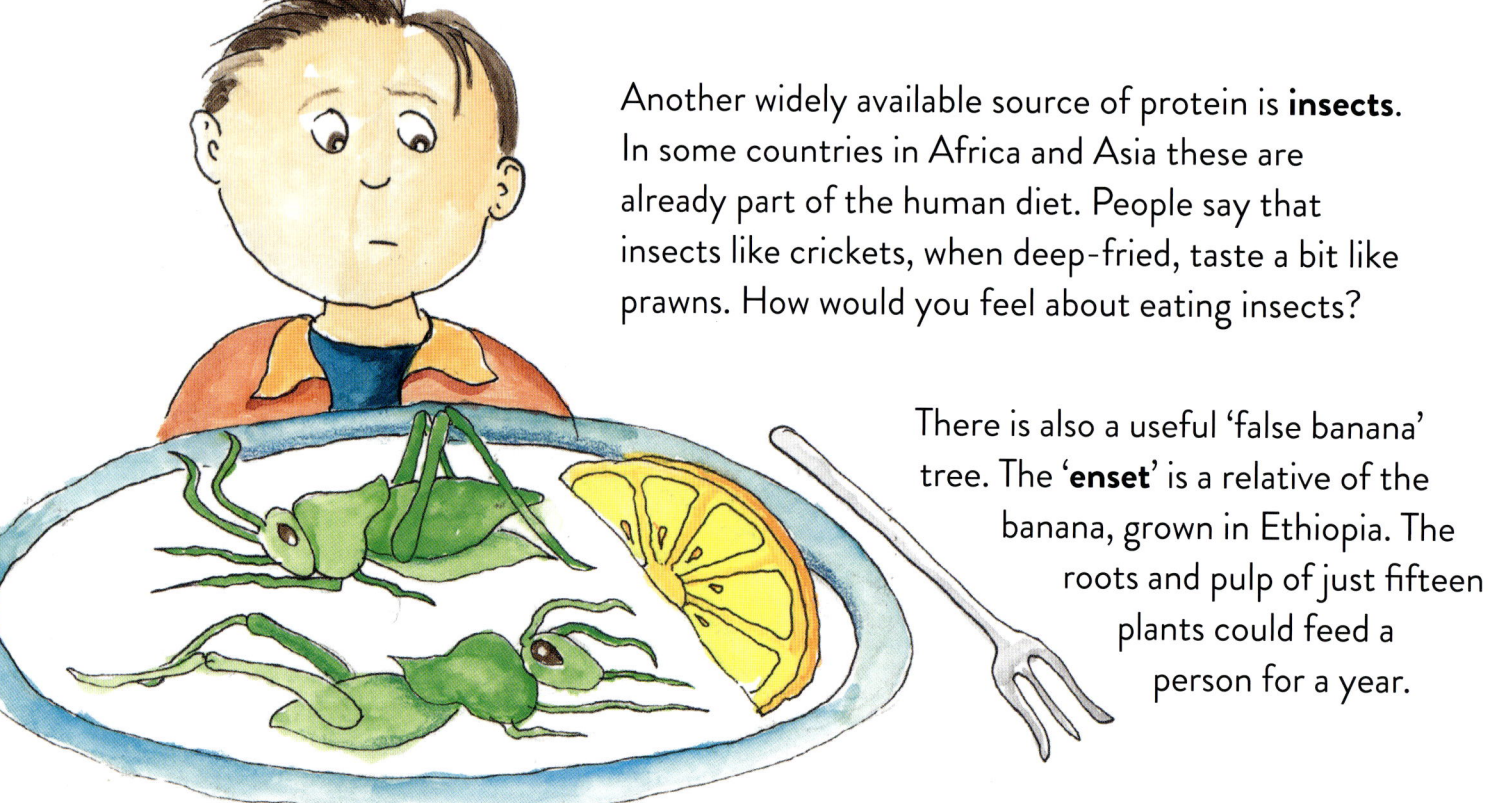

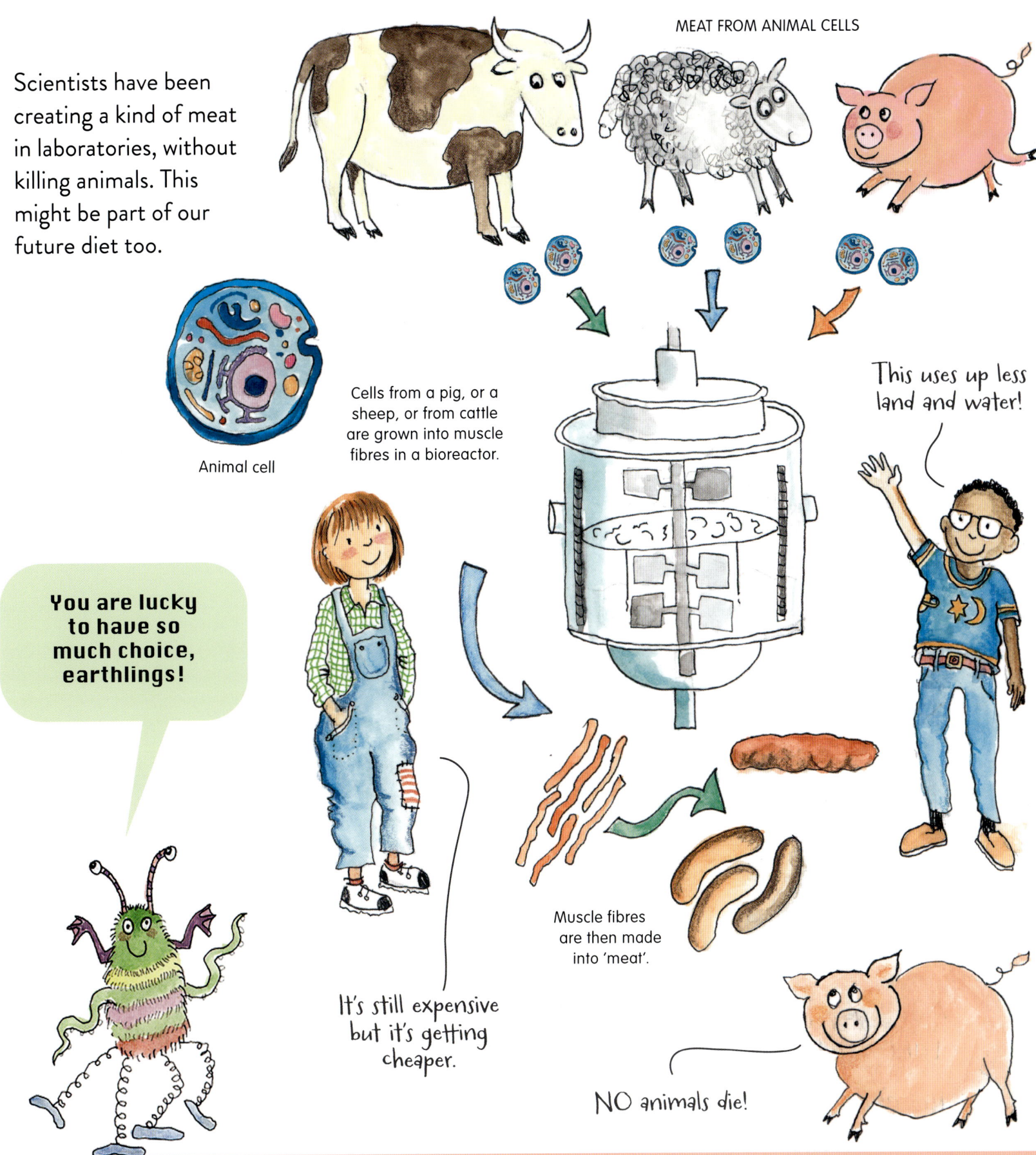

Scientists have been creating a kind of meat in laboratories, without killing animals. This might be part of our future diet too.

MEAT FROM ANIMAL CELLS

Animal cell

Cells from a pig, or a sheep, or from cattle are grown into muscle fibres in a bioreactor.

This uses up less land and water!

You are lucky to have so much choice, earthlings!

It's still expensive but it's getting cheaper.

Muscle fibres are then made into 'meat'.

NO animals die!

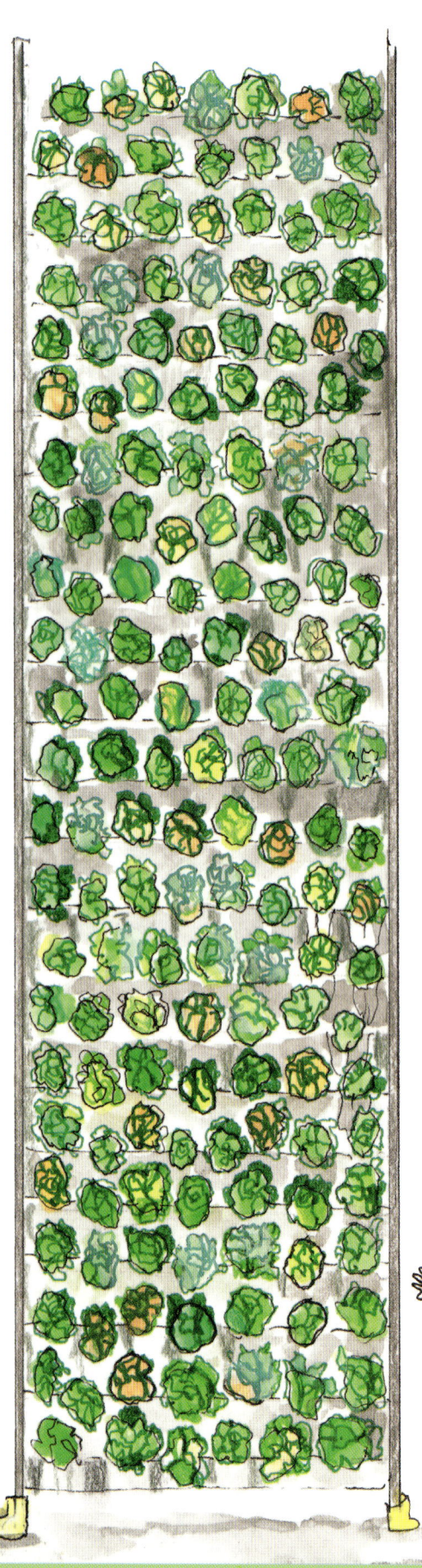

Feed the world

What have we learned about food?

Whatever else, we shouldn't waste it. Governments should build refrigeration units and weatherproof barns so that no food is left to go bad before it is eaten.

But ordinary families can help too, by using all the food they buy and recycling things like peels, outer leaves of vegetables and eggshells, for garden compost or local food-waste schemes.

We need to build irrigation plants or flood barriers to combat climate change, so we can go on growing and raising enough food on our planet for all the people on it. Vertical farming, which takes up far less land, is being developed in some countries.

This is vertical farming! How many cabbages do you think there are in this tall space?

RICE IS NICE

MORE FRUIT

LESS SUGAR

EAT WELL!

I LOVE PEAS

MORE VEG!

Food needs to be affordable – for everyone. Governments and food producers must not make greedy profits but producers should be paid fairly by supermarkets. And people should be paid enough for their work so they can afford to buy food.

If we all take action and make changes to what we eat and how we live, we CAN grow and raise enough food for everyone on the planet, so that no one goes hungry.

FOOD FOR ALL!

COME ON, EARTHLINGS! YOU CAN DO IT!

ENJOY LOVELY FOOD

EAT LOCAL FOOD

FOOD is FUN! (AND TASTY)

VEGAN PETS!

SAVE the BEE!

NO SILLY PACKAGING

EAT LESS MEAT

NO WASTE

SAVE the WORM!

SLOW FOOD

Glossary

Lots of interesting and useful words here!

Billion	A thousand million
Climate change	Long-term changes in temperature and weather
Coeliac disease	A condition that means the person can't digest gluten in any form; it makes them very ill
Carnivore	An animal that eats mainly other animals
Crops	Plants grown for human food, animal feed, fibres, oil, flowers and shrubs, rubber and tobacco
Drought	Times when there is no rain for months or even years
Famine	A serious lack of affordable food, so that people are in danger of starving to death
Flood	Such a high rise in rain that rivers overflow or seas rise
Food Aid	The help that richer countries give to poorer ones after natural disasters or wars
Food allergy	A bad physical reaction to some foods, ranging from a rash to death
Food bank/food pantry	A place where people who can't afford to buy food can get it free
Gluten	An ingredient of wheat and some other grains
Herbivore	An animal that eats only plants
Livestock	Farmed animals like cows, sheep, goats, pigs, hens and ducks, who provide people with meat, milk and eggs
Manure	Poo produced by animals, which can be spread on fields to fertilise the land where crops are grown
Methane	A gas produced by the stomachs of animals like cows and sheep, who graze on grass all day
Million	A thousand thousand
Organic	Grown or raised without chemicals
Omnivore	An animal or human who eats everything
Pescatarian	Someone who eats fish but not meat
Staple	The food of a region which is eaten almost every day
Vegan	Someone who eats no meat, fish, eggs, milk or cheese
Vegetarian	Someone who eats no meat, fish or seafood
Vertical farming	Growing plants up tall supporting structures so that farmers can get a crop many times bigger while using only a small amount of land